T. A. Goodwin

Lovers Three Thousand Years Ago as Indicated by the Song

of Solomon

T. A. Goodwin

Lovers Three Thousand Years Ago as Indicated by the Song of Solomon

ISBN/EAN: 9783337008130

Printed in Europe, USA, Canada, Australia, Japan

Cover: Foto ©Thomas Meinert / pixelio.de

More available books at **www.hansebooks.com**

LOVERS

THREE THOUSAND YEARS AGO

AS INDICATED BY

THE SONG OF SOLOMON

BY

REV. T. A. GOODWIN, D. D.

———

CHICAGO
THE OPEN COURT PUBLISHING COMPANY
1895

PREFACE.

THE author of this little book does not claim to have just discovered that the Song of Solomon is a love-story in verse. That was suggested by Bible-scholars many years ago, and it has been very generally accepted by the scholarship of to-day. But in all the literature upon the subject, whether in the form of monographs, or of articles in magazines, or reviews, or encyclopædias, there is not found a single presentation of it in a form which would allow it to be read in its real character. These discussions are all in the form of critical expositions of the text, so that in most of them the text appears only in fragments. The plan of this book is to eliminate all textual criticism and to restore the text to the form which made the poem a treasure with the ancient Hebrews, and which, when thus read, will make it as dear to every true lover to-day as it was when first read and recited three thousand years ago.

CONTENTS.

THE HISTORICAL IMPORT OF THE POEM.

TO THE common reader of the Bible, and little less to the careful Bible student, the book known as the Song of Solomon is a perpetual enigma. Not seeming to meet any of the supposed purposes for which the Bible was written, many good men, including many whose business it is to teach Bible truth, seldom if ever read it as they read other Scriptures, and not a few hold that its incorporation into the sacred canon is somebody's blunder. It is not difficult to account for this, when we call to mind the once prevailing opinion of what the Bible is and what it is for. Being found in that collection of histories and prophecies and songs, which by the way of pre-eminence we call the Bible, and which is held sacred by devout and learned Christians and Hebrews as the repository of correct doctrine and of safe rules of conduct ; and seeming to contain nothing that may be regarded as either doctrinal or didactic, Bible students as well as the common Bible reader have been put to their wits' end to find a place for it.

During the Middle Ages the dogma of the plenary inspiration of the Scriptures was promulgated with such pertinacity, that long after the Bible became the property of the common people this figment held a place in their thoughts.   Even as late as the days of King James this was the case to such an extent that the translators whom he had chosen to prepare an author-ised version so rendered Paul's language to Timothy as to read, "All Scripture is given by inspiration of God."   This practically settled the question with the common reader, so that the Song of Solomon and the Book of Ruth were placed on a level with the proph-ecies of Isaiah and Daniel and the writings of Moses and of David, as being designed to teach doctrine or to administer reproof, or to instruct in right living.

All down the ages following, individual scholars protested against this rendering, but their protests went unheeded, as unworthy of acceptance in the face of the opinion of the learned commission of the king, who, in the popular thought, were little if any less in-spired than the sacred writers themselves.   This com-pelled Bible scholars to adapt the "Song" to the general purpose of inspired Scripture, so that it might be profitable in some way "for doctrine, for reproof, for correction, and for instruction in righteousness."

One can hardly review with complacency the many schemes of Bible teachers to bring this book into line with Isaiah and Daniel and the Psalms, so that with them and other inspired books it may refer to the Messiah, and may instruct the Church in things spiritual. By some it has been regarded as an allegory, by others a parable, whose hidden meaning might be guessed at, if not comprehended. In keeping with this thought almost from the first edition of the authorised version, the editors of the several editions have seemed to vie with each other in ingenious suggestions as to the signification of this or that sentence or paragraph ; and preachers, from the unlearned rustic, in ministering to his uneducated and emotional flock, to the profound doctor of divinity in his city pulpit, preaching to men of culture, have found spiritual "instruction" in such passages as "I have put off my coat, how can I put it on?" "Thy teeth are like a flock of sheep." "The head upon thee is like Carmel." "We have a little sister and she hath no breasts."

The sermons may all have been good enough and may have conveyed important lessons to the hearers, but they might have been "founded" as well upon some passage in Milton or Shakespeare or Dante as upon these. Not the least objectionable use of this Song, or parts of it, is that made by hymn-writers. Who can enumerate the hymns that find their chief attraction in poetic changes upon the Rose of Sharon, the Lily of the Valley, the Turtle Dove, the One Altogether Lovely, or some other similar phrase in this book? If all the hymns which are inspired by some passage from the Song of Solomon were expurgated from some collections of hymns there would be little

left worth singing.   Many of them are beautiful, but
their beauty does not consist in the thought of the text
as it stands in its proper meaning.

It is positively ludicrous, if the following exposition of the Song be the correct one, to read the head-
ings of the chapters and the running titles in our common family Bibles, which are intended to give a clue
to the meaning of the text.   They run thus: "The
Church's love for Christ," "She confesseth her deformity," "Christ directs her to the Shepherd's tent,
and showeth His love to her," "Having a taste of
Christ's love, is sick of love," and so on, calling the
lover's passionate description of his affianced, "Christ
showing the graces of the Church, and His love towards
her," though elsewhere they have the Church confess-
ing her deformity.

It is plain that any intelligent exposition of this
book, or, for that matter, of any part of the sacred
Scriptures, must be along the line which repudiates
the figment of Plenary Inspiration, at whose doors
most, if not all, the obscurity which envelops this
Song of Solomon lies, as well as do many indefensi-
ble dogmas, which have the same paternity. Not only
does the Bible nowhere make such a claim for itself,
but the structure of the book as a whole, and of its
contents taken separately, are evidences against the
assumption.

The advent of the revised version, the product of
a ripe scholarship that cannot be gainsaid, has greatly

aided in the proper understanding of this Song, as well as of many other parts of our sacred Scriptures. There is a far-reaching difference between "All Scripture is given by inspiration of God," as the authorised version has it, and "Every Scripture, inspired of God," as it appears in the revised version. The scope of this treatise does not require the elaboration of this difference. It is sufficient for its purpose to state that the plain inference is that Paul and the Jews of his period, and of course the Christians also, held that some portions of the sacred writings, as they then possessed them, were not so inspired as to be specially profitable for doctrine or for reproof, or for instruction in righteousness.

The assumption that Solomon was himself the author of the Song has very little to sustain it. That it is called the Song of Solomon, or the Song of Songs, which is Solomon's, proves nothing. He could not have written it, unless the remorse which possessed him towards the close of his misspent life, and which led him to pronounce that life a failure, implied more than remorse usually does. The author was not even a friend of Solomon's. The whole poem is a scathing rebuke to all his social and domestic methods. It is quite as likely to be the product of some man or woman a hundred years or more later than Solomon's time, and more likely to be that of a woman than of a man, judging from the tender pathos of many portions of the poem which very few men could exhibit. The

author, whether male or female, whether living near
Solomon's time or much later, gave birth to this un-
dying poem and then died leaving nothing else worth
preserving, not even a name.

It was probably founded upon some fact in the life
of that lecherous king, which had been transmitted
through generations by authentic history or by tradi-
tion or both, out of which the gifted poet built this
most admirable production as Longfellow built his
Miles Standish out of the traditions and history of the
early pilgrim fathers. Its being called the Song of
Solomon no more proves or even suggests that Solomon was its author than will the *Song of Hiawatha*
prove or suggest three thousand years hence that Hiawatha was the author of the poem which this genera-
tion knows was written by another.

Neither is it difficult to account for its place in the
sacred canon. Books in those days were few and only
those that struck the popular heart had the distinction of a reproduction through the expensive process
of being copied by hand; hence few ever reached the
second edition, much less a general circulation through
multiplied copies, so as to be preserved through succeeding ages.

When Ezra and Nehemiah returned to Jerusalem
after the long captivity in Babylon their first duty was
of course to provide for immediate physical wants;
hence they addressed themselves heroically to the re-
building of the temple and the reconstruction of the

walls of Jerusalem. When this had been done they found another work of not less piety and patriotism, though so much less ostentatious as hardly to find mention in the annals of the Hebrew people. When they and those who followed them looked around they found that most of the literature of their nation had been "lost by reason of the war." To recover this as much as possible seems to have been a chief aim of Nehemiah, hence he set about "founding a library, gathering together the acts of the kings and the writings of the prophets, and of David and the epistles of the kings" (2 Macc., 2, 13).

It needed not to be specifically mentioned by the historian of that period that this lover of the literature of the fathers included other songs than the songs of David, for others are included in the collection of pious songs called the Psalms. In their quest they found among other books this poem, and it, too, was incorporated into the national library, and thus it was preserved through the succeeding ages, and thus it has come down to us.

It had then been preserved through probably not less than four hundred years in manuscript alone, and had probably been recited during all those years of tribulation, in which, according to the prophet, the nation had been "scattered and peeled and meeted out and trodden down." From the Assyrian captivity ten of the tribes never returned sufficiently organised to retain their tribeship. Finding this book thus preserved they gave it a place in their collection and thus it became a part of the Sacred Writings. And no wonder. It had vindicated its right to immortality. When read or recited as the Hebrew people read and recited it, before it had been allegorised out of all significance, it could not fail to interest every true heart. It delineates the triumph of true love over all the allurements of wealth and lust in such a manner as to strike all pure men and women as above praise.

It was never claimed by those compilers or for them by others until long after the coming of Christ that all these books were inspired in the sense inspiration is used in modern theological discourse. It was only a collection of history and prophecy and song. It was the beginning of a public library which was by no means completed during the lives of its founders, but was continued through succeeding generations by the Great Synagogue. At no time was it claimed for this collection as a whole that it had such divine sanction that whatever it contained should have the authority of a "Thus saith the Lord."

In the time of the Maccabees this library was to be "read with favor and attention" (Prologue to Ecclesiasticus), and we have no record that as a whole at any time down to and including the times of Christ it had any other sacredness than that veneration which is due to any collection of ancient writings. Hence the significance of Paul's distinction in his letter to Timothy, between the Scriptures which were given by inspiration and those that make no claim to that origin, when speaking of what is profitable for doctrines and reproof and instruction which is in righteousness.

It matters nothing one way or the other that neither Christ nor any of his disciples ever quoted from this book, so far as the meagre records of their sayings show; for many other books of Ezra's canon are in the same category and some of these books are of much historic importance. It is much more significant as relating to the question of inspiration that they quoted from books then in common use, no copy of which has come down to us, among our Sacred Writings. No book is extant which details the contention between Moses and Jannes and Jambres, nor have we any part of the Prophecy of Enoch from which Jude quoted as something with which the people of his time were familiar. It is even more significant in relation to the plenary inspiration of the sacred writings of apostolic times that when Christ opened the understanding of his two disciples who met him on their way to Emmaus, that they might understand the Scriptures that he quoted only from "the law of Moses and the Prophets and the Psalms."

That such a book should be placed in the "Library" of Ezra and Nehemiah and be preserved in it through succeeding centuries is no wonder. Neither is it any wonder that centuries later, when the Christian fathers were compiling their collection "to set forth in order the things which we believe," this thrilling book should be retained, though not conspicuously adapted to doctrine, or reproof, or instruction. The Bible as a light to human feet along every pathway of life would be incomplete without it. We have the personification of faith in the story of Abraham ; of patience, in the story of Job ; of filial love, in the story of Ruth ; of endurance, in the story of Moses ; and here we have a photograph of ardent conjugal love, the most holy sentiment of humanity, in the story of a humble shepherdess and her equally humble and faithful lover ; a constant rebuke to that pietism which teaches that ardent conjugal love is only a sensual passion which must be foresworn or tethered if one would attain the highest type of moral character—a most detestable heresy.

THE CHARACTER OF THE POEM.

THE true place in literature for this Song of Songs is that of a Love Story in verse. To call it a drama is hardly to classify it intelligibly to popular thought, yet it partakes of most of the elements of a drama, and is more of a drama than anything else. It certainly belongs to the drama family. If it were allowable to build a word out of recognised material at hand, I would call it a drama-et. While it lacks the scenic touches which are necessary to adapt it to the stage, yet when read or rendered even in the less pretentious form of a dialogue it is necessary to change time and place and the *dramatis personæ*, in order to catch its significance.

In the following rendering I have followed in the main the text of the revised version as bringing out more nearly the meaning of the original, and because the metrical arrangement is more suggestive of poetry. But in comparing even this with the original the Bible student feels at every step, as he feels a thousand times elsewhere in such a comparison, that the revisers were too much handicapped by a well-meant

agreement at the start, to retain the phraseology of
the authorised version wherever possible without too
much injury to the sense of the original. Here as elsewhere they have confessedly often failed to give the
best possible rendering, perpetuating thereby not a
few incorrect notions if not also in some cases some
doubtful doctrines.

While therefore scholars readily recognise many
changes for the better in the rendering of this Song by
the revisers, they also detect not a few instances where
the meaning might have been greatly improved by a
departure from the old phraseology. Take, for example, Chapter 7, verse 2, in the Song. It is not a
matter of delicacy merely which induces me to substi-
tute the word *waist* for the word *navel*, and the word
body for the word *belly*. There is nothing in the navel
alone to suggest a round goblet full of wine, while, by
the aid of a little poetic fancy, the waist may suggest
it. Neither is there anything in the belly alone, as
that word is now used by all English speaking peo-
ples, to suggest a heap of wheat encircled with lilies,
while a well-formed body, as that word is now used to
include the central and principal parts of the human
frame, may easily suggest the figure used. These
several words in the original mean what the translators have given as their English equivalents, but they
mean also *waist* and *body* respectively. I am sure that
the reader will appreciate the change.

Again, the Hebrew text can never be translated

into our language literally so as to be intelligible. For that matter no dead language can, and very few living languages; hence in all translations explanatory words are frequently used of necessity. In the following rendering I have availed myself of this necessary prerogative, supplying adverbs and prepositions and other words that seem necessary to bring out the meaning of the original by making the text correspond with the idiom of the English language. For example at Chapter 2, verse 6, the heroine is made to say both in the old and in the new versions: " His left hand *is* under my head and his right hand *doth* embrace me." There is no verb in the original from which our *is* can be obtained and the tense of the verb to be supplied can as well be in the future as in the present; besides, it avoids a false statement not justifiable even by poetic licence, for as a matter of fact no left hand was under her head nor was any right hand embracing her. But even this change of tense still leaves the meaning obscure, or rather leaves the sentence meaningless. The shepherdess is protesting against the caresses of the lecherous Solomon and saying of her shepherd lover: "*Only* his left hand shall sustain my head and *only* his right hand shall embrace me ;" meaning that none but her virtuous Shulammite shepherd shall be allowed the liberties of a lover ; hence, in addition to changing the tense I have supplied the necessary adverb.

In all cases I have omitted such distinctive marks as italics and quotations. The curious reader may easily compare the text here given with the text of the revised version if he wishes to see how far and wherein I have departed from it ; while the scholarly reader may compare it with the original Hebrew if he wishes to see what liberties I have taken in order to bring out the meaning of the poem. I have also wholly ignored the artificial chaptering and versing of the text. In no other way can the connexion be preserved which is necessary to a right understanding of the book.

It will be observed that I have not followed the suggestions of those who would dignify the poem by making it a drama and introducing acts and scenes accordingly. To so construe it involves too many difficulties. One of these is so great that no two of those who have attempted to divide it into acts have ever agreed where one act ends and another begins, neither can they agree as to the *dramatis personæ*. I have simply sought to restore it to its original form as nearly as that can be ascertained after the lapse of so many centuries, as it was read or recited by the common people, three thousand years ago, whether they were captives by the rivers of Babylon or of Assyria, or were slaves on the banks of their own Jordan, with only such equipments as might be improvised for the occasion, by slaves and captives. Classifying it with the unpretentious dialogue places it within the reach of the common people, who could read or recite it without the expensive paraphernalia of the theatre.

The scene opens in the gorgeous country seat of the wealthy and dissipated King Solomon, where were houses and vineyards and orchards and gardens, with much silver and gold and cattle and men servants and women servants and all the peculiar wealth of kings, including many women and much wine. It was early in the reign of that famous monarch. His harem at that time had only sixty women who posed as wives, and only eighty who were classed as concubines, whatever the difference between them may have been. Later these were increased to seven hundred wives and three hundred concubines. It was in the process of multiplying these wives that the incidents of the story belong.

The heroine of the story is a beautiful sun-burnt maiden, who had been brought from her country-home in Northern Palestine to this accumulation of splendors. To assume, as some do, that she had been captured by a band of brigands and taken by force to the king's harem, is to do violence to every known law of human nature. Unwilling captives would soon transform a harem into a hell from which the would-be lord would flee for dear life. Not one of the possible pleasures of such an accumulation of the means of sensual enjoyments could be found there. Solomon was too wise even in his most abandoned moods to do such violence to every law of lust. The harem was not a prison for unwilling captives, to be obtained or retained by force, but a place with such attractions as

to make it a desirable home as compared with the ordinary home-life of the women of Palestine at that
time.   We must not form our estimate of the lot of a
second or a second-hundredth wife of that period by
our views of polygamy to-day.   Frequent and devas-
tating wars made the disparity in numbers between
males and females very great, and the honor of moth-
erhood removed from a multiplicity of wives most of
what now makes polygamy abhorrent.

The harem was replenished through the agency of
procurers, whose business it was to travel through the
country and induce handsome women to become in-
mates.   Human nature is not so changed in these
three thousand years that we need suppose that the
methods of these procurers were essentially different
from the methods of men and women of their class to-
day.   Possibly in no case was their purpose fully dis-
closed at the first.   The hard lot of women, especially
in the rural districts, made it easy then, as it is too
easy now, for a plausible man or woman to persuade
young women to exchange their country surroundings
and hard work for the easier lot of an inmate of a
king's palace.   Once there, under whatever induce-
ment, they were put into the hands of governesses,
whose duty it was to gain their consent to yield to the
lust of the king, either as a wife or concubine.   Light
domestic duties and luxurious living were combined
until the consent was obtained ;   the king himself
taking no prominent part in these preparatory pro-

ceedings, probably knowing nothing of the novitiate until her consent had been obtained to become his wife.

Our heroine was a rustic girl whose hard life was not most agreeable. In her earlier girlhood she had been detailed to the duty of guarding the family flock. This had brought her into the company of neighboring shepherds, among whom was a handsome young man, between whom and her there had grown a strong mutual attachment. She had two half-brothers who were displeased with this love-affair. Nothing else proving effectual, in order to break it off, they transferred their sister from the flocks to the vineyard, subjecting her to exposure to the hot sun and to the harder work of dressing the vines. While in rebellion against this oppression, she was visited by one or more of the procurers for Solomon's harem. It was not difficult, under the circumstances, to persuade her that in the palace of the king she would find better treatment and more satisfactory remuneration than she was receiving as a vine-dresser. How long she had been in her new home when the story begins, need not matter; it had been long enough for those who had her in charge to venture to unfold to her the ultimate purpose for which she had been brought into the king's family.

The next most important person, the hero of the story, is the Shulammite shepherd, the devoted lover of the brave young woman, who so persistently re-

fused to abandon him, and to exchange his love for
what was proposed to her as a wife of the lecherous
king.

The next most important characters are a trio of
middle-aged women, from among the wives of the
king, the governesses to whose charge she had been
committed, who are called in the poem "Daughters of
Jerusalem," or "Daughters of Zion." This young
shepherdess was from the tribe of Issachar. Her home
was far away. The country of her birth was fertile,
and abounded in vineyards and flocks, but her people
were humble, though thrifty; hence the splendor of
the city-life, and especially of the king's palace, could
but have a charm for them, which made them regard
the woman who wore a part of these splendors as
entitled to such distinction as is implied in those
titles.

We may readily suppose that in ordinary cases the
task of these women was not a difficult one. There
was so little in the humdrum of domestic life in the
country to satisfy the laudable aspirations of a spirited
woman and so many attractions in the surroundings of
the court that it must have been an easy task usually,
under the loose notions of that period concerning the
sacredness of marriage, to gain the consent of the new-
comer to the conditions of her remaining ; hence the
stubborn and persistent resistance of this Shulammite
shepherdess was a surprise to them.

This is all beautifully set forth in the poem as well as is the honorable womanly course of the trio towards her when they comprehend her situation.

The progress of inauguration into this new life was a simple one.   The new victim, who had been allured to the palace under the impression that she was to have some honorable and remunerative employment about the extensive establishment, was clothed in better raiment, and fed on better food, and regaled on more and better wine than she had been accustomed to, until her governesses had gained her consent to forever abandon her country home and the associations and lover of her childhood, for the pomp and splendors of a queen.   The luxuriant appointments of the palace; its baths, its tables, and its wardrobes usually did the work; hence it is untenable to assume, as some do, that Solomon himself at any time addresses the maiden in words of adulation or entreaty, or addresses her at all.

Solomon himself plays but a passive and merely a coincidental part in the poem.   He is made to be personally unconscious of what is going on in his own behalf in the palace.   He appears in the distance in a royal pageant, but not in any sense for the purpose of settling the question under discussion by the women and the maiden, though the women readily seize upon the event to supplement their own arguments.   He was carried in his splendid car of state, accompanied by one of his queens, and was greeted with loud plaudits.   What effect this had upon the shepherdess appears in the poem.

The half-brothers of the shepherdess play a sorry part in the affair, both at the beginning and at the ending, and the neighbors turn out to congratulate the lovers on the successful issue of the struggle when they return to the scenes of their earlier courtship.

THE SONG OF SONGS.

THE poem begins abruptly. The women, her keepers, had just feasted her at the family table of the King's household. Wine had constituted a conspicuous part of the bill of fare, and the women had praised the luxuries which the King's family enjoyed, contrasting it with the simple fare of a vine-dresser among the hills of Issachar; assuring her that all this was at the service of a wife of the King. The purpose for which she had been enticed from her country home and from the shepherd youth whom she loved, was now for the first time broached to her. It was not to be a domestic in the King's palace, but to become one of his wives, already numbering sixty. At this she promptly rebelled. She would never consent to the lustful embraces of one whom she could not love, though he be a king, and informing the women she had a lover among the shepherds of Shulam she breaks out :

"Let him kiss me with the kisses of his mouth."

Then turning to the lover himself who in the dialogue is made to be opportunely present she says :

''For thy love is better than wine.
    Thine ointments have a goodly fragrance,
    Thy name is as ointment poured forth,
    Therefore do maidens love thee.
    Draw me after thee, let us run !
    The King hath brought me into his harem,
    We will greatly rejoice in thee,
    We will esteem thy caress more than wine,
    Rightly do the maidens love thee.''

Addressing the women she continues :

''I am black but I am comely,
    O, ye daughters of Jerusalem ;
    Like the tents of Kedar,
    Like the pavilions of Solomon.
    Despise me not because I am swarthy,
    Because the sun hath scorched me,
    My half-brothers were incensed against me,
    They made me keeper of the vineyards,
    Mine own vineyard I have not kept.''

Again addressing the lover, she says :

''Tell me, thou whom my soul loveth,
    Where thou feedest thy flock, where thou makest it to rest at
        noon,
    For why should I be as a woman veiled,
    Beside the flocks of thy companions ? ''

· The answer of the women to this frantic outburst of love and fidelity is a compliment to the woman-heart that had survived all the blandishments of the royal household.   It at once awakened recollections of earlier days when the voice and society of some

rustic lover was all the world to them, but from whom
they had been allured by the displays of ease and lux-
ury in the King's palace, and whose love they had
bartered away for the dubious honors and the unsatis-
fying pleasures of the King's court and the King's
chamber. Moved to sympathy by her appeals to them
and to her lover ; and in their woman-hearts wishing
she might escape the fate that had befallen themselves,
they reply :

> "If thou knowest not, O thou fairest among women !
>   Get thee again to the footsteps of thy flock,
>   And feed thy kids beside the shepherd's tent."

The shepherd now addresses his lover, returning
the personal compliment she had so handsomely paid
him :

> "I have compared thee, O, my love !
>   To a steed in Pharaoh's chariots.
>   Thy cheeks are comely with plaits of hair,
>   Thy neck with strings of jewels."

The women, to neutralise the effect of this compliment to her beauty interpose, saying ,

> "We will make thee plaits of gold,
>   With studs of silver, if thou become a queen."

The shepherdess, addressing the women, pays her
lover this beautiful compliment :

> "While the King sat at his table,
>   My spikenard sent forth its fragrance.
>   But my beloved is unto me as a bundle of myrrh,

> That lieth between my breasts;
> My beloved is unto me as a cluster of camphire,
> From the vineyards of Engedi."

The following playful interchange of compliments between the two lovers cannot be excelled in any love story, nor often in real life. It is both delicate and extravagant. He begins :

> "Behold thou art fair, my love, behold thou art fair,
> Thine eyes are as doves' eyes."

To this she replies :

> "Behold thou art fair, my beloved, yea, very pleasant,
> Also our couch is green."

In answer to this allusion to the place of their out-door courtships he refers to the cedars and firs under which they sat :

> "The beams of our house are cedars,
> And our rafters are firs."

There is a spice of humor in her self-praise :

> "I am a rose of Sharon,
> A lily of the valley."

But he is equal to the occasion and turns her self-compliment to good account by accepting it with emphasis :

> "As a lily among the thorns,
> So is my beloved among the daughters."

Turning to the women the shepherdess continues to compliment her lover and avow her fidelity to him :

" As an apple-tree among the trees of the forest,
  So is my beloved among the sons.
  I sat under his shadow with great delight,
  And his fruit was sweet to my taste.
  He brought me to his wine-house,
  And his banner over me was love.
  Stay me with grapes, comfort me with apples,
  For I am sick of love.
  Only his left hand shall sustain my head,
  And only his right hand shall embrace me.
  I adjure you, O daughters of Jerusalem,
  By the roes and by the hinds of the field,
  That you stir not up nor awaken love,
  Until it please."

This appeal to the women to not attempt to force love is both pathetic and philosophic. Love finds its own time and object without the intermeddling of others. The shepherdess continues abstractedly:

" The voice of my beloved ! behold he cometh,
  Leaping upon the mountains, skipping upon the hills,
  My beloved is like a roe or a young hart.
  Behold ! he standeth behind our wall,
  He cometh in at the window,
  He peepeth through the lattice.
  My beloved spake and said unto me :
  Rise up my love, my fair one, and come away,
  For lo ! the winter is past,
  The rain is over and gone ;
  The flowers appear upon the earth,
  The time of the singing of birds has come
  And the voice of the turtle is heard in our land.
  The fig-tree ripens her figs

And the vines are in blossom ;
They give forth their fragrance."

Turning to the shepherd again, she says :

"Arise, my love, my fair one, and come away,
O my dove ! thou art in the clefts of the rocks, in the covert
     of the steep place ;
Let me see thy face, let me hear thy voice,
For charming is thy voice and thy features are lovely.
Take us the foxes, the little foxes that ruin the vineyards,
For our vineyards are in blossom."

Turning to address the women, she continues :

"My beloved is mine and I am his,
He feedeth his flocks among the lilies
Until the day be cool and the shadows flee away."

Again addressing the shepherd, she says :

"Turn, my beloved, and be thou like a roe or a young hart
Upon the mountains of Bether."

She relates a dream :

"By night, on my bed, I sought him whom my soul loveth,
I sought him but I found him not,
I said I will rise now and go about the city,
In the streets and in the broad ways,
I will seek him whom my soul loveth :
I sought him in my dream but I found him not.
The watchmen that go about the city found me ;
I said to them, saw ye him whom my soul loveth ?
I was but a little passed from them
When I found him whom my soul loveth ;
I caught him and would not let him go
Until he had brought me to my mother's house,
Into the chamber of her that gave me birth."

Again, turning to the women she charges them not to attempt to force love.

> "I adjure you, O daughters of Jerusalem,
>   By the roes and the hinds of the field,
>   That ye stir not up nor awaken love
>   Until it please."

At this point a royal cortége is seen in the distance. It had no necessary connexion with the work of reconciling this pure country girl to the proposed new conditions, but it offered a new argument, as they supposed; hence they called attention to it and especially to the fact that one of the queens was a partaker with the King of all its magnificence. As it was only one of the frequent parades of the King they sought to excite her womanly love of display by the assurance that a like honor awaited her if she would consent to become a queen also. One of the women calls attention to it by asking:

> "Who is this that cometh up out of the wilderness like pillars
>   of smoke?
>   Perfumed with myrrh and frankincense,
>   With all the powders of the merchant?"

A second woman :

> "Behold it is the litter of Solomon;
>   Three-score mighty men are about it,
>   Of the mighty men of Israel.
>   They all handle the sword and are expert in war,
>   Every man hath his sword on his thigh,
>   Because of fear in the night."

The third woman takes it up :

"King Solomon made himself a car of state
Of the wood of Lebanon.
He made the posts thereof of silver,
The bottoms thereof of gold, the seat thereof of purple.
In the midst thereof sits a sparkling beauty
From the daughters of Jerusalem."

The shepherdess's answer to all this is one of the finest touches in the whole poem. Reduced to plain prose it is equivalent to saying : if such splendors have attractions for you, you are welcome to them all, for they do not move me :

"Go forth, O daughters of Zion, and behold King Solomon
With the crown wherewith his mother crowned him in the
day of his espousals ;
And in the day of the gladness of his heart."

The following rhapsody of the shepherd lover has no rival in any language for hyperbole. Compared with it Shakespeare's most famous,

"But you, O you,
So perfect and so peerless are created
Of every creature's best,"

seems quite tame. It is such touches of nature that preserved this poem through those centuries of war and captivity and which ultimately gave it a place in the sacred literature of the restored Hebrews, and still later, a place among the sacred books of Christians ; and now, after three thousand years many a gray-headed sire will read it and recall the time in his own experience when, as far as he was able, he indited just such a sonnet to a pair of dove's eyes and scarlet lips, and a pretty neck with teeth and temples to match.

" Behold thou art fair, my love, behold thou art fair,
  Thine eyes are as dove's eyes behind thy veil,
  Thy hair is as a flock of goats
  That lie along the side of Gilead ;
  Thy teeth are like a flock of sheep newly shorn,
  Which come up from the washing,
  Whereof every one of them hath twins,
  And not one of them is bereaved.
  Thy lips are like a thread of scarlet
  And thy mouth is comely ;
  Thy cheek is like a side of a pomegranate
  Behind thy veil.
  Thy neck is like the tower of David, builded for an armory,
  Wherein there hang a thousand bucklers
  And all the shields of mighty men.
  Thy two breasts are like two twin fawns of a roe
  Which feed among the lilies."

The shepherdess, pretending with true womanly affectation to desire no more of such adulation, seeks to interrupt him by saying :

"Until the day be cool and the shadows lengthen,
  I will get me to the mountain of myrrh
  And to the hill of frankincense."

But he was not to be silenced. The interruption only intensified his speech. Beginning at the same beginning as before he becomes much more violent :

" Thou art fair my love,
  And there is no spot in thee.

Come with me from Lebanon, my spouse,
With me from Lebanon.
Look upon me from the top of Amena,
From the top of Senir and Hermon,
From the depths of the lion's den,
From the mountains of leopards.
Thou hast ravished my heart, my sister, my spouse,
Thou hast ravished my heart with one glance of thine eyes,
With one of the ringlets that encircle thy neck.
How pleasant is thy love, my sister, my spouse;
How much better is thine embrace than wine!
And the odor of thy perfumes than all manner of spices.
Thy lips, O my spouse, distil odors as the honey-comb,
Honey and milk are concealed under thy tongue,
And the fragrance of thy garments is like the fragrance of
        Lebanon,
A garden enclosed, is my sister, my spouse,
A spring shut up, a fountain sealed;
A paradise, where the pomegranate blossoms, together with
        precious fruits,
Camphire with spikenard plants,
Spikenard and saffron,
Calamus and cinnamon with all manner of sweet-smelling
        plants,
Myrrh and aloes with all the chief spices.
Thou art a fountain of gardens,
A well of living waters,
And flowing streams from Lebanon.

Awake, O north wind and come thou south,
Blow upon my garden that the fragrance thereof may flow
        out!"

The shepherdess answers :

"Let my beloved come into his garden,
And eat his precious fruits."

The shepherd :

"I have come into my garden, my sister, my spouse,
I have gathered my myrrh and my spices,
I have eaten my honey-comb with my honey
I have drunk my wine with my milk.

Eat, O friends,
Drink, yea, drink abundantly."

The shepherdess, that she may the more impress her keepers, the women, that it was cruel to separate her from her devoted lover, relates another recent dream :

"I was asleep, but my heart was awake,
It was the voice of my beloved.   As he knocked,
He said, open to me, my sister, my love, my dove, my per-
fect one ;
For my head is covered with dew,
My locks with the drops of the night.
To tease him I said, I have put off my coat, how shall I put
it on ?
I have washed my feet, why should I soil them ?
At this my beloved withdrew his hand from the latch,
And my bosom quivered thereat.
I then rose up to open to my beloved,
And my hands dropped with myrrh,
And my fingers with liquid myrrh
Overflowed upon the handle of the lock.

When I opened to my beloved,
Behold my beloved had withdrawn himself, and was gone.
(When I spake to him I was bereft of reason.)
I sought him, but I could not find him ;
I called, but he gave me no answer ;
I dreamed the watchmen that go about the city found me
They smote me, they wounded me,
And the keepers on the wall took away my veil :

I adjure you, O ye daughters of Jerusalem, if ye find my
    beloved,
His mouth is most sweet, yea, his person is altogether lovely.
That you tell him I am dying of love."

Again the enthusiasm of the young shepherdess aroused the sympathy of the women, who had not forgotten experiences in their own earlier lives not greatly unlike this, hence, instead of longer persisting in attempts to persuade their ward to consent to become such as they were, they offer assistance to her, or, at least, they wish to know more about the young man she had left behind ; hence they ask :

" What is thy beloved more than another beloved,
O thou fairest among women ?
What is thy beloved more than another beloved,
That thou shouldst so adjure us ? "

This gave the shepherdess occasion to describe him as she viewed him, and, unless love was blind, he was worthy her love :

' My beloved is white and ruddy,
The fairest among ten thousand,
His head is as the most fine gold,

His locks are curling and black as a raven,
His eyes are as doves' eyes, reflecting in the water-brooks,
Washing in milk and sitting in full streams,
His cheeks are as a bed of balsam, as towers of perfumes,
His lips are as lilies, dropping liquid myrrh,
His hands are as rings of gold set with beryl,
His reins are as ivory work overlaid with sapphires,
His legs are as pillars of marble set on pedestals of gold,
His appearance is as Lebanon, beautiful as the cedars,

Such is my beloved, such is my friend,
O daughters of Jerusalem."

This enthusiastic description of the absent lover only increased the interest which the women felt in their ward, and they wish to hear more about him hence they ask ;

"Whither is thy beloved gone,
O thou fairest among women ?
Whither is thy beloved turned aside,
That we may seek him with thee ?"

The shepherdess :

"My beloved has gone down to his garden to the beds of balsam,
To feed his flocks in the garden and to gather lilies.
I am my beloved's and he is mine,
My beloved who feedeth his flocks among the lilies."

The shepherd again praises the beauty of his spouse, repeating, as would be natural, much that he had said before :

"Thou art beautiful, O my love, as Tirzah,
Charming as Jerusalem,

Terrible as an army in battle.
Turn away thine eyes from me,
For they have overcome me.
Thy hair is like a flock of goats
Lying along the side of Gilead.
Thy teeth are like a flock of sheep
Which have just been washed,
Whereof every one hath twins,
And none is bereaved among them.
Thy cheek is as a slice of pomegranate
Behind thy veil."

To show the great wrong there would be in pressing one so dear to him into a harem already crowded, he says:

" There are in the household of Solomon already three-score
    queens, and four-score concubines,
And young maidens without number.
My dove, my perfect one, is but one ;
She is the only one of her mother ;
She is the choice one of her that gave her birth.
The young saw her and called her blessed,
The queens and the concubines saw her and they praised
    her saying :
Who is she that looketh forth like the morning
Fair as the moon,
Clear as the sun,
Terrible as an army in battle ? "

The shepherdess here narrates a reverie :

" In fancy I went down to the garden of nuts,
To see the green plants of the valley;
To see whether the vine budded,
And the pomegranates were in flower.

Before I was aware, my desire set me
Among the chariots of my people."

The interest of the women in the absent lover was so aroused that they desire to see him, hence they say:

"Return, O Shulammite shepherd,
Return, return, that we may see thee."

The shepherdess rebukes their idle curiosity by saying :

"Why wish ye to look upon the Shulammite,
As upon the dance of angels at Mahanaim ? "

The scene of the following is in the ladies' toilette. The women, notwithstanding the sympathy they had expressed for the unwilling victim of their scheme, determined to make one more effort to overcome her objections. This time they resort to flattery by praising her personal beauty. She had just come from the bath and had put on only her slippers, when they began, hoping to so arouse her vanity that she would at once discard her country lover :

" How beautiful are thy feet in sandals, O prince's daughter !
Thy round thighs are like ornaments,
The work of the hand of a cunning workman.
Thy waist is like a round goblet,
Wherein aromatic wine is abundant.
Thy body is like a heap of wheat,
Encircled with lilies.
Thy two breasts are like two fawns
That are twins of a roe.
Thy neck is like a tower of ivory.

> Thine eyes are like the pools of Heshbon by the gate of
>   Bathrabbim ;
> Thy nose is like the side of the tower of Lebanon,
> Which looketh towards Damascus ;
> Thine head upon thee is like Carmel,
> And the locks of thine head are like threads of purple ;
> The King will be held captive in the tresses thereof.
> How fair and how charming art thou,
> O love, for delights !
> Thy stature is like a palm-tree,
> And thy breasts are like to clusters of grapes."

The shepherd interposes with his claim to all these charms :

> "I said I will climb up into my palm-tree,
> I will take hold of the branches thereof ;
> Thy breasts shall be to me as clusters of grapes,
> And the odor of thy breath like apples ;
> And thy mouth as the best of wine,
> That goeth down sweetly for my beloved,
> Causing the lips of those that are asleep to speak."

The shepherdess answers the appeal of the women, and she consents to the proposition of the lover, thus settling the question by saying :

> "I am my beloved's,
> And his desire is towards me."

Thereupon the lover proposes that they leave the palace and go forth :

> "Come, my beloved, let us go forth into the fields,
> Let us lodge in the villages,
> Let us get up early and go to the vines.
> Let us see whether the vine-stalks have budded,

And the tender grapes appear,
Whether the pomegranate be in flower ;
There will I give thee my caress.
The mandrakes give forth fragrance,
And at our gates are all manner of fruits, both new and old
Which I have laid up for thee, O beloved !" *1720*

The shepherdess, feeling hampered by the conventionalities of the times, which did not allow her to embrace her lover in public, yet tolerated the osculation and caressing of a brother, replies :

"O that thou wert as my brother,
  Who nursed at the breast of my mother,
  So that when I should meet thee without I could embrace
    thee,
  And none would despise me therefor!
  I would lead thee and bring thee into my mother's house,
  Where thou mightest instruct me,
  And I would cause thee to drink of spiced wine,
  Of the sweet wine of my pomegranates."

Turning to the women, she says :

"Only his left hand shall sustain my head,
  And only his right hand shall embrace me.
  I adjure you, O daughters of Jerusalem,
  That ye stir not up nor awaken love, until it please."

The women at last consent to her leaving the palace in company with her shepherd lover, who escorted her to the home of her mother. The neighbors seeing them returning, ask :

"Who is this that cometh up from the wilderness,
  Leaning upon her beloved ?"

Before reaching the house they stop a moment under the apple-tree, which had often listened to their mutual avowals of love.   Once there, seated upon the rustic seat they had so often occupied, he recalls other meetings at that sacred spot, and says :

" Under this apple-tree I first aroused thy love,"

Then, pointing to the house beyond the garden, he says :

" In yonder house thy mother conceived thee,
    There she was in travail and there she gave thee birth ;
    Now set me as a seal upon thine heart, as a bracelet upon
        thine arm,
    For love is strong as death ;
    Jealousy is cruel as the grave,
    Its flames are flames of fire,
    Its arrows the fire of Jehovah.
    Great waters cannot quench love,
    And rivers cannot overwhelm it."

Then, delicately alluding to the late experience of his faithful lover in resisting the blandishments of the King's palace, he adds :

" If a man would offer all his substance for love
    He would only reap confusion."

The two half-brothers now appear.   They had lost none of their opposition to this love-affair.   At first they had sought to break it off by taking their sister from the care of the sheep, which afforded too many opportunities for the lovers to meet each other, and putting her to the harder work of dressing the family vineyard. This failing, they had connived at, if they had not suggested and promoted, the scheme of getting her into Solomon's harem. For their sister to be a wife of the King, though only one of many, was much preferable, in their minds, to her being the wife of a humble shepherd, even if some personal grudge against their young neighbor had not something to do in the case. But in this they were again baffled, and they find her once more in the family home, more devoted than ever to her rustic lover. Their last hope now is to belittle their sister, and to postpone, if not to entirely prevent, the marriage, by alleging that she was too young, and by insinuating other and grave impediments. They derisively ask what shall be the wedding presents in the case of a marriage, as well as insinuate unfitness for wifehood. They say:

> "We have a little sister,
> And she hath no breasts ;
> What shall we do for our sister
> In the day when she shall be spoken for ?
> If she be a wall,
> We will build upon her a turret of silver ;
> If she be a door,
> We will inclose her with boards of cedar."

Her answer is both womanly and defiant. Recognising that she is in no sense under obligations to them for what she is, and what she hopes to be soon, the bride of one who will be to her a wall of defence, she says :

" I have been a wall,
  And my breasts have been towers,
  Hence I was in my lover's eyes as a woman that finds peace-

  Solomon had a vineyard at Baal-hamon ;
  He let out the vineyard to keepers,
  Every one to bring, as rent, a thousand of silver.
  My vineyard is in front of me.
  Thou, O Solomon, may have the thousand,
  And thy keepers may have two hundred."

The shepherd :

  " Thou that dwellest in the gardens,
  The companions are listening to thy voice,
  Cause me to hear it."

The shepherdess :

  " Make haste, my beloved,
  And be thou like to a roe or a young hart
  Upon the mountain of spices."

Ordinary love stories end in the marriage of the
chief characters. This does not, but it is easy to see
that such constancy on the part of each, under such
inducements to unfaithfulness, can end no otherwise
after reaching the point where the poem leaves them.
Though when read as an allegory, this poem is utterly
meaningless ; yet when read as a love story in verse,
no pure man or woman can rise from its reading without having been benefited. It touches at many points
the experience of true lovers in all the ages, and hence
its immortality.

Inevitably, a poem of so great antiquity, abounding in Orientalisms, must contain many historic, geographic, and social allusions, which it is difficult, if not impossible, to understand to-day. All parts of the old Hebrew Scriptures are in the same category. What if we cannot understand what was meant in its time by "the dance of angels at Mahanaim," or why it was interesting to be looked upon from the lion's den or the mountains of leopards? It is sheer folly to seek a meaning for these in allegory or parable. But, given the instinctive drawings of a virtuous youth and a virtuous maiden of congenial tastes, we have the key to this inimitable poem. Though therefore we may not understand all its allusions, when we read it as a poem intended to set forth a victory of faithful love in the form of a dialogue, which may easily be acted by amateurs, we are compelled to concede its right to a place in our sacred collection of the books which constitute our Bible. It can never cease to be of interest to all pure minds. No better lesson is taught in any Bible story, nor ever can be, while the maximum of human happiness is found only in households where true love reigns supreme; and not the least lesson it teaches is the unchanging elements of love—the same three thousand years ago as now.

www.ingramcontent.com/pod-product-compliance
Lightning Source LLC
Chambersburg PA
CBHW032133080426
42733CB00008B/1056